HUGHIE

Eugene O'Neill # HUGHIE

New Haven

Yale University Press

Printed in the United States of America by
The Murray Printing Co., Westford, Massachusetts.

Library of Congress catalog card number: 58–11259.

ISBN: 0–300–00806–6 (cloth), 0–300–02881–4 (paper).

THE EUGENE O'NEILL COLLECTION was founded at the Yale University Library
in 1931 by Carlotta Monterey O'Neill. It includes notes, photographs, and the
manuscripts of plays, among them *Hughie*. All royalties from the sale of the Yale
editions of this book go to Yale University for the benefit of the Eugene O'Neill
Collection, for the purchase of books in the field of drama, and for the
establishment of Eugene O'Neill Scholarships in the Yale School of Drama.

15   14   13   12   11   10   9   8   7   6

Characters

"Erie" Smith, a teller of tales

A Night Clerk

Scene

The desk and a section of lobby of a small hotel on a West Side street in midtown New York. It is between 3 and 4 A.M. of a day in the summer of 1928.

It is one of those hotels, built in the decade 1900–10 on the side streets of the Great White Way sector, which began as respectable second class but soon were forced to deteriorate in order to survive. Following the First World War and Prohibition, it had given up all pretense of respectability, and now is anything a paying guest wants it to be, a third class dump, catering to the catch-as-catch-can trade. But still it does not prosper. It has not shared in the Great Hollow Boom of the twenties. The Everlasting Opulence of the New Economic Law has overlooked it. It manages to keep running by cutting the overhead for service, repairs, and cleanliness to a minimum.

The desk faces left along a section of seedy lobby with shabby chairs. The street entrance is off-stage, left. Behind the desk are a telephone switchboard and the operator's stool. At right, the usual numbered tiers of mailboxes, and above them a clock.

The NIGHT CLERK *sits on the stool, facing front, his back to the switchboard. There is nothing to do. He is not thinking. He is not sleepy. He simply droops and stares acquiescently at nothing. It would be discouraging to glance at the clock. He knows there are several hours to go before his shift is over. Anyway, he does not need to look at clocks. He has been a night clerk in New York hotels so long he can tell time by sounds in the street.*

He is in his early forties. Tall, thin, with a scrawny neck and jutting Adam's apple. His face is long and narrow, greasy with perspiration, sallow, studded with pimples from ingrowing hairs. His nose is large and without character. So is his mouth. So are his ears. So is his thinning brown hair, powdered with dandruff. Behind horn-rimmed spectacles, his blank brown eyes contain no discernible expression. One would say they had even forgotten how it feels to be bored. He wears an ill-fitting blue serge suit, white shirt and collar, a blue tie. The suit is old and shines at the elbows as if it had been waxed and polished.

Footsteps echo in the deserted lobby as someone comes in from the street. The Night Clerk rises wearily. His eyes remain empty but his gummy lips part automatically in a welcoming The-Patron-Is-Always-Right grimace, intended as a smile. His big uneven teeth are in bad condition.

ERIE SMITH *enters and approaches the desk. He is about the same age as the Clerk and has the same pasty, perspiry, night-life complexion. There the resemblance ends. Erie is around medium height but appears shorter because he is stout and his fat legs are too short for his body. So are his fat arms. His big head squats on a neck which seems part of his beefy shoulders. His face is round, his snub nose flattened at the tip. His blue eyes have drooping lids and puffy pouches under them. His sandy hair is falling out and the top of his head is bald. He walks to the desk with a breezy, familiar air, his gait a bit waddling because of his short legs. He carries a Panama hat and mops his face with a red and blue silk handkerchief. He wears a light grey suit cut in the extreme, tight-waisted, Broadway mode, the coat open to reveal an old and faded but expensive silk shirt in a shade of blue that sets teeth on edge, and a gay red and blue foulard tie, its knot stained by perspiration. His trousers are held up by a braided brown leather belt with a brass buckle. His shoes are tan and white, his socks white silk.*

In manner, he is consciously a Broadway sport and a Wise Guy—the type of small fry gambler and horse player, living hand to mouth on the fringe of the rackets. Infesting corners, doorways, cheap restaurants, the bars of minor speakeasies, he and his kind imagine they are in the Real Know, cynical oracles of the One True Grapevine.

Erie usually speaks in a low, guarded tone, his droop-lidded eyes suspiciously wary of nonexistent eavesdroppers. His face is set in the prescribed pattern of gambler's dead pan. His small, pursy mouth is always crooked in the cynical leer of one who possesses superior, inside information, and his shifty once-over glances never miss the price tags he detects on everything and everybody. Yet there is something phoney about his characterization of himself, some sentimental softness behind it which doesn't belong in the hard-boiled picture.

Erie avoids looking at the Night Clerk, as if he resented him.

ERIE
Peremptorily.

Key.

> *Then as the Night Clerk gropes with his memory—grudgingly.*

Forgot you ain't seen me before. Erie Smith's the name. I'm an old timer in this fleabag. 492.

NIGHT CLERK
In a tone of one who is wearily relieved when he does not have to remember anything—he plucks out the key.

492. Yes, sir.

ERIE
Taking the key, gives the Clerk the once-over. He appears not unfavorably impressed but his tone still holds resentment.

How long you been on the job? Four, five days, huh? I been off on a drunk. Come to now, though. Tapering off. Well, I'm glad they fired that young squirt they took on when Hughie got sick. One of them fresh wise punks. Couldn't tell him nothing. Pleased to meet you, Pal. Hope you stick around.

He shoves out his hand. The Night Clerk takes it obediently.

NIGHT CLERK
With a compliant, uninterested smile.

Glad to know you, Mr. Smith.

ERIE
What's your name?

NIGHT CLERK
As if he had half forgotten because what did it matter, anyway?

Hughes. Charlie Hughes.

ERIE
Starts.

Huh? Hughes? Say, is that on the level?

Charlie Hughes.

ERIE

Well, I be damned! What the hell d'you know about that!
Warming toward the Clerk.
Say, now I notice, you don't look like Hughie, but you remind me
of him somehow. You ain't by any chance related?

NIGHT CLERK

You mean to the Hughes who had this job so long and died recently? No, sir. No relation.

ERIE
Gloomily.
No, that's right. Hughie told me he didn't have no relations left
—except his wife and kids, of course.
He pauses—more gloomily.
Yeah. The poor guy croaked last week. His funeral was what
started me off on a bat.
Then boastfully, as if defending himself against gloom.
Some drunk! I don't go on one often. It's bum dope in my book.
A guy gets careless and gabs about things he knows and when he
comes to he's liable to find there's guys who'd feel easier if he
wasn't around no more. That's the trouble with knowing things.
Take my tip, Pal. Don't never know nothin'. Be a sap and stay
healthy.

*His manner has become secretive, with sinister undertones.
But the Night Clerk doesn't notice this. Long experience
with guests who stop at his desk in the small hours to talk
about themselves has given him a foolproof technique of
self-defense. He appears to listen with agreeable sub-
missiveness and be impressed, but his mind is blank and*

*he doesn't hear unless a direct question is put to him, and
sometimes not even then. Erie thinks he is impressed.*

But hell, I always keep my noggin working, booze or no booze.
I'm no sucker. What was I sayin'? Oh, some drunk. I sure hit the
high spots. You shoulda seen the doll I made night before last.
And did she take me to the cleaners! I'm a sucker for blondes.

*He pauses—giving the Night Clerk a cynical, con-
temptuous glance.*

You're married, ain't you?

NIGHT CLERK

*Long ago he gave up caring whether questions were per-
sonal or not.*

Yes, sir.

ERIE

Yeah, I'd'a laid ten to one on it. You got that old look. Like
Hughie had. Maybe that's the resemblance.

He chuckles contemptuously.

Kids, too, I bet?

NIGHT CLERK

Yes, sir. Three.

ERIE

You're worse off than Hughie was. He only had two. Three, huh?
Well, that's what comes of being careless!

*He laughs. The Night Clerk smiles at a guest. He had
been a little offended when a guest first made that crack
—must have been ten years ago—yes, Eddie, the oldest,
is eleven now—or is it twelve? Erie goes on with good-
natured tolerance.*

Well, I suppose marriage ain't such a bum racket, if you're made
for it. Hughie didn't seem to mind it much, although if you want
my low-down, his wife is a bum—in spades! Oh, I don't mean

cheatin'. With her puss and figure, she'd never make no one except she raided a blind asylum.

> *The Night Clerk feels that he has been standing a long time and his feet are beginning to ache and he wishes 492 would stop talking and go to bed so he can sit down again and listen to the noises in the street and think about nothing. Erie gives him an amused, condescending glance.*

How old are you? Wait! Let me guess. You look fifty or over but I'll lay ten to one you're forty-three or maybe forty-four.

NIGHT CLERK

I'm forty-three.

> *He adds vaguely.*

Or maybe it is forty-four.

ERIE

> *Elated.*

I win, huh? I sure can call the turn on ages, Buddy. You ought to see the dolls get sored up when I work it on them! You're like Hughie. He looked like he'd never see fifty again and he was only forty-three. Me, I'm forty-five. Never think it, would you? Most of the dames don't think I've hit forty yet.

> *The Night Clerk shifts his position so he can lean more on the desk. Maybe those shoes he sees advertised for fallen arches— But they cost eight dollars, so that's out— Get a pair when he goes to heaven. Erie is sizing him up with another cynical, friendly glance.*

I make another bet about you. Born and raised in the sticks, wasn't you?

NIGHT CLERK

> *Faintly aroused and defensive.*

I come originally from Saginaw, Michigan, but I've lived here in the Big Town so long I consider myself a New Yorker now.

*This is a long speech for him and he wonders sadly why
he took the trouble to make it.*

ERIE

I don't deserve no medal for picking that one. Nearly every guy
I know on the Big Stem—and I know most of 'em—hails from the
sticks. Take me. You'd never guess it but I was dragged up in
Erie, P-a. Ain't that a knockout! Erie, P-a! That's how I got my
moniker. No one calls me nothing but Erie. You better call me
Erie, too, Pal, or I won't know when you're talkin' to me.

NIGHT CLERK

All right, Erie.

ERIE

Atta Boy.
    He chuckles.
Here's another knockout. Smith is my real name. A Broadway guy
like me named Smith and it's my real name! Ain't that a knockout!
    *He explains carefully so there will be no misunderstand-
    ing.*
I don't remember nothing much about Erie, P-a, you understand
—or want to. Some punk burg! After grammar school, my Old
Man put me to work in his store, dealing out groceries. Some
punk job! I stuck it till I was eighteen before I took a run-out
powder.
    *The Night Clerk seems turned into a drooping wax-
    work, draped along the desk. This is what he used to
    dread before he perfected his technique of not listening:
    The Guest's Story of His Life. He fixes his mind on his
    aching feet. Erie chuckles.*
Speaking of marriage, that was the big reason I ducked. A doll
nearly had me hooked for the old shotgun ceremony. Closest I
ever come to being played for a sucker. This doll in Erie—Daisy's

14

her name—was one of them dumb wide-open dolls. All the guys give her a play. Then one day she wakes up and finds she's going to have a kid. I never figured she meant to frame me in particular. Way I always figured, she didn't have no idea who, so she holds a lottery all by herself. Put about a thousand guys' names in a hat— all she could remember—and drew one out and I was it. Then she told her Ma, and her Ma told her Pa, and her Pa come round looking for me. But I was no fall guy even in them days. I took it on the lam. For Saratoga, to look the bangtails over. I'd started to be a horse player in Erie, though I'd never seen a track. I been one ever since.

With a touch of bravado.

And I ain't done so bad, Pal. I've made some killings in my time the gang still gab about. I've been in the big bucks. More'n once, and I will be again. I've had tough breaks too, but what the hell, I always get by. When the horses won't run for me, there's draw or stud. When they're bad, there's a crap game. And when they're all bad, there's always bucks to pick up for little errands I ain't talkin' about, which they give a guy who can keep his clam shut. Oh, I get along, Buddy. I get along fine.

> *He waits for approving assent from the Night Clerk, but the latter is not hearing so intently he misses his cue until the expectant silence crashes his ears.*

NIGHT CLERK
Hastily, gambling on "yes."

Yes, Sir.

ERIE
Bitingly.

Sorry if I'm keeping you up, Sport.

With an aggrieved air.

Hughie was a wide-awake guy. He was always waiting for me to roll in. He'd say, "Hello, Erie, how'd the bangtails treat you?" Or,

"How's luck?" Or, "Did you make the old bones behave?" Then I'd tell him how I'd done. He'd ask, "What's new along the Big Stem?" and I'd tell him the latest off the grapevine.

He grins with affectionate condescension.

It used to hand me a laugh to hear old Hughie crackin' like a sport. In all the years I knew him, he never bet a buck on nothin'.

Excusingly.

But it ain't his fault. He'd have took a chance, but how could he with his wife keepin' cases on every nickel of his salary? I showed him lots of ways he could cross her up, but he was too scared.

He chuckles.

The biggest knockout was when he'd kid me about dames. He'd crack, "What? No blonde to-night, Erie? You must be slippin'." Jeez, you never see a guy more bashful with a doll around than Hughie was. I used to introduce him to the tramps I'd drag home with me. I'd wise them up to kid him along and pretend they'd fell for him. In two minutes, they'd have him hanging on the ropes. His face'd be red and he'd look like he wanted to crawl under the desk and hide. Some of them dolls was raw babies. They'd make him pretty raw propositions. He'd stutter like he was paralyzed. But he ate it up, just the same. He was tickled pink. I used to hope maybe I could nerve him up to do a little cheatin'. I'd offer to fix it for him with one of my dolls. Hell, I got plenty, I wouldn't have minded. I'd tell him, "Just let that wife of yours know you're cheatin', and she'll have some respect for you." But he was too scared.

He pauses—boastfully.

Some queens I've brought here in my time, Brother—frails from the Follies, or the Scandals, or the Frolics, that'd knock your eye out! And I still can make 'em. You watch. I ain't slippin'.

He looks at the Night Clerk expecting reassurance, but the Clerk's mind has slipped away to the clanging bounce of garbage cans in the outer night. He is thinking: "A job I'd like. I'd bang those cans louder than they do! I'd wake up the whole damned city!" Erie mutters disgustedly to himself.

Jesus, what a dummy!

He makes a move in the direction of the elevator, off right front—gloomily.

Might as well hit the hay, I guess.

NIGHT CLERK

Comes to—with the nearest approach to feeling he has shown in many a long night—approvingly.

Good night, Mr. Smith. I hope you have a good rest.

But Erie stops, glancing around the deserted lobby with forlorn distaste, jiggling the room key in his hand.

ERIE

What a crummy dump! What did I come back for? I shoulda stayed on a drunk. You'd never guess it, Buddy, but when I first come here this was a classy hotel—and clean, can you believe it?

He scowls.

I've been campin' here, off and on, fifteen years, but I've got a good notion to move out. It ain't the same place since Hughie was took to the hospital.

Gloomily.

Hell with going to bed! I'll just lie there worrying—

He turns back to the desk. The Clerk's face would express despair, but the last time he was able to feel despair was back around World War days when the cost of living got so high and he was out of a job for three months. Erie leans on the desk—in a dejected, confidential tone.

Believe me, Brother, I never been a guy to worry, but this time I'm on a spot where I got to, if I ain't a sap.

17

NIGHT CLERK

In the vague tone of a corpse which admits it once over-heard a favorable rumor about life.

That's too bad, Mr. Smith. But they say most of the things we worry about never happen.

His mind escapes to the street again to play bouncing cans with the garbage men.

ERIE

Grimly.

This thing happens, Pal. I ain't won a bet at nothin' since Hughie was took to the hospital. I'm jinxed. And that ain't all— But to hell with it! You're right, at that. Something always turns up for me. I was born lucky. I ain't worried. Just moaning low. Hell, who don't when they're getting over a drunk? You know how it is. The Brooklyn Boys march over the bridge with bloodhounds to hunt you down. And I'm still carrying the torch for Hughie. His checking out was a real K.O. for me. Damn if I know why. Lots of guys I've been pals with, in a way, croaked from booze or something, or got rubbed out, but I always took it as part of the game. Hell, we all gotta croak. Here today, gone tomorrow, so what's the good of beefin'? When a guy's dead, he's dead. He don't give a damn, so why should anybody else?

But this fatalistic philosophy is no comfort and Erie sighs.

I miss Hughie, I guess. I guess I'd got to like him a lot.

Again he explains carefully so there will be no mis-understanding.

Not that I was ever real pals with him, you understand. He didn't run in my class. He didn't know none of the answers. He was just a sucker.

He sighs again.

But I sure am sorry he's gone. You missed a lot not knowing Hughie, Pal. He sure was one grand little guy.

18

He stares at the lobby floor. The Night Clerk regards him with vacant, bulging eyes full of a vague envy for the blind. The garbage men have gone their predestined way. Time is that much older. The Clerk's mind remains in the street to greet the noise of a far-off El train. Its approach is pleasantly like a memory of hope; then it roars and rocks and rattles past the nearby corner, and the noise pleasantly deafens memory; then it recedes and dies, and there is something melancholy about that. But there is hope. Only so many El trains pass in one night, and each one passing leaves one less to pass, so the night recedes, too, until at last it must die and join all the other long nights in Nirvana, the Big Night of Nights. And that's life. "What I always tell Jess when she nags me to worry about something: 'That's life, isn't it? What can you do about it?' " *Erie sighs again—then turns to the Clerk, his foolishly wary, wise-guy eyes defenseless, his poker face as self-betraying as a hurt dog's—appealingly.*

Say, you do remind me of Hughie somehow, Pal. You got the same look on your map.

But the Clerk's mind is far away attending the obsequies of night, and it takes it some time to get back. Erie is hurt —contemptuously.

But I guess it's only that old night clerk look! There's one of 'em born every minute!

NIGHT CLERK
His mind arrives just in time to catch this last—with a bright grimace.

Yes, Mr. Smith. That's what Barnum said, and it's certainly true, isn't it?

ERIE
Grateful even for this sign of companionship, growls.

Nix on the Mr. Smith stuff, Charlie. There's ten of *them* born every minute. Call me Erie, like I told you.

NIGHT CLERK
Automatically, as his mind tiptoes into the night again.
All right, Erie.

ERIE
Encouraged, leans on the desk, clacking his room key like a castanet.
Yeah. Hughie was one grand little guy. All the same, like I said, he wasn't the kind of guy you'd ever figger a guy like me would take to. Because he was a sucker, see—the kind of sap you'd take to the cleaners a million times and he'd never wise up he was took. Why, night after night, just for a gag, I'd get him to shoot crap with me here on the desk. With *my* dice. And he'd never ask to give 'em the once-over. Can you beat that!
He chuckles—then earnestly.
Not that I'd ever ring in no phoneys on a pal. I'm no heel.
He chuckles again.
And anyway, I didn't need none to take Hughie because he never even made me knock 'em against nothing. Just a roll on the desk here. Boy, if they'd ever let me throw 'em that way in a real game, I'd be worth ten million dollars.
He laughs.
You'da thought Hughie woulda got wise something was out of order when, no matter how much he'd win on a run of luck like suckers have sometimes, I'd always take him to the cleaners in the end. But he never suspicioned nothing. All he'd say was "Gosh, Erie, no wonder you took up gambling. You sure were born lucky."
He chuckles.
Can you beat that?
He hastens to explain earnestly.

Of course, like I said, it was only a gag. We'd play with real jack, just to make it look real, but it was all my jack. He never had no jack. His wife dealt him four bits a day for spending money. So I'd stake him at the start to half of what I got—in chicken feed, I mean. We'd pretend a cent was a buck, and a nickel was a fin and so on. Some big game! He got a big kick out of it. He'd get all het up. It give me a kick, too—especially when he'd say, "Gosh, Erie, I don't wonder you never worry about money, with your luck."

He laughs.

That guy would believe anything! Of course, I'd stall him off when he'd want to shoot nights when I didn't have a goddamned nickel.

He chuckles.

What laughs he used to hand me! He'd always call horses "the bangtails," like he'd known 'em all his life—and he'd never seen a race horse, not till I kidnaped him one day and took him down to Belmont. What a kick he got out of that! I got scared he'd pass out with excitement. And he wasn't doing no betting either. All he had was four bits. It was just the track, and the crowd, and the horses got him. Mostly the horses.

With a surprised, reflective air.

Y'know, it's funny how a dumb, simple guy like Hughie will all of a sudden get something right. He says, "They're the most beautiful things in the world, I think." And he wins! I tell you, Pal, I'd rather sleep in the same stall with old Man o' War than make the whole damn Follies. What do you think?

> NIGHT CLERK
> *His mind darts back from a cruising taxi and blinks be-wilderedly in the light: "Say yes."*

Yes, I agree with you, Mr.—I mean, Erie.

ERIE

With good-natured contempt.

Yeah? I bet you never seen one, except back at the old Fair Grounds in the sticks. I don't mean them kind of turtles. I mean a real horse.

> *The Clerk wonders what horses have to do with any-thing—or for that matter, what anything has to do with anything—then gives it up. Erie takes up his tale.*

And what d'you think happened the next night? Damned if Hughie didn't dig two bucks out of his pants and try to slip 'em to me. "Let this ride on the nose of whatever horse you're betting on tomorrow," he told me. I got sore. "Nix," I told him, "if you're going to start playin' sucker and bettin' on horse races, you don't get no assist from me."

> *He grins wryly.*

Was that a laugh! Me advising a sucker not to bet when I've spent a lot of my life tellin' saps a story to make 'em bet! I said, "Where'd you grab this dough? Outa the Little Woman's purse, huh? What tale you going to give her when you lose it? She'll start breaking up the furniture with you!" "No," he says, "she'll just cry." "That's worse," I said, "no guy can beat that racket. I had a doll cry on me once in a restaurant full of people till I had to promise her a diamond engagement ring to sober her up." Well, anyway, Hughie sneaked the two bucks back in the Little Woman's purse when he went home that morning, and that was the end of that.

> *Cynically.*

Boy Scouts got nothin' on me, Pal, when it comes to good deeds. That was one I done. It's too bad I can't remember no others.

> *He is well wound up now and goes on without noticing that the Night Clerk's mind has left the premises in his sole custody.*

Y'know I had Hughie sized up for a sap the first time I see him. I'd just rolled in from Tia Juana. I'd made a big killing down there and I was lousy with jack. Came all the way in a drawing room, and I wasn't lonely in it neither. There was a blonde movie doll on the train—and I was lucky in them days. Used to follow the horses South every winter. I don't no more. Sick of traveling. And I ain't as lucky as I was—

Hastily.

Anyway, this time I'm talkin' about, soon as I hit this lobby I see there's a new night clerk, and while I'm signing up for the bridal suite I make a bet with myself he's never been nothin' but a night clerk. And I win. At first, he wouldn't open up. Not that he was cagey about gabbin' too much. But like he couldn't think of nothin' about himself worth saying. But after he'd seen me roll in here the last one every night, and I'd stop to kid him along and tell him the tale of what I'd win that day, he got friendly and talked. He'd come from a hick burg upstate. Graduated from high school, and had a shot at different jobs in the old home town but couldn't make the grade until he was took on as night clerk in the hotel there. Then he made good. But he wasn't satisfied. Didn't like being only a night clerk where everybody knew him. He'd read somewhere—in the Suckers' Almanac, I guess—that all a guy had to do was come to the Big Town and Old Man Success would be waitin' at the Grand Central to give him the key to the city. What a gag that is! Even I believed that once, and no one could ever call me a sap. Well, anyway, he made the break and come here and the only job he could get was night clerk. Then he fell in love —or kidded himself he was—and got married. Met her on a sub-way train. It stopped sudden and she was jerked into him, and he put his arms around her, and they started talking, and the poor boob never stood a chance. She was a sales girl in some punk de-partment store, and she was sick of standing on her dogs all day, and all the way home to Brooklyn, too. So, the way I figger it, knowing Hughie and dames, she proposed and said "yes" for him, and married him, and after that, of course, he never dared stop being a night clerk, even if he could.

He pauses.

Maybe you think I ain't giving her a square shake. Well, maybe I ain't. She never give me one. She put me down as a bad influence, and let her chips ride. And maybe Hughie couldn't have done no better. Dolls didn't call him no riot. Hughie and her seemed happy enough the time he had me out to dinner in their flat. Well, not happy. Maybe contented. No, that's boosting it, too. Resigned comes nearer, as if each was givin' the other a break by thinking, "Well, what more could I expect?"

Abruptly he addresses the Night Clerk with contemptuous good nature.

How d'you and your Little Woman hit it off, Brother?

NIGHT CLERK

His mind has been counting the footfalls of the cop on the beat as they recede, sauntering longingly toward the dawn's release. "If he'd only shoot it out with a gunman some night! Nothing exciting has happened in any night I've ever lived through!" He stammers gropingly among the echoes of Erie's last words.

Oh—you mean *my* wife? Why, we get along all right, I guess.

ERIE

Disgustedly.

Better lay off them headache pills, Pal. First thing you know, some guy is going to call you a dope.

But the Night Clerk cannot take this seriously. It is years since he cared what anyone called him. So many guests have called him so many things. The Little Woman has, too. And, of course, he has, himself. But that's all past. Is daybreak coming now? No, too early yet. He can tell

by the sound of that surface car. It is still lost in the night.
Flat wheeled and tired. Distant the carbarn, and far away
the sleep. Erie, having soothed resentment with his wise-
crack, goes on with a friendly grin.

Well, keep hoping, Pal. Hughie was as big a dope as you until I
give him some interest in life.

Slipping back into narrative.

That time he took me home to dinner. Was that a knockout! It
took him a hell of a while to get up nerve to ask me. "Sure,
Hughie," I told him, "I'll be tickled to death." I was thinking, I'd
rather be shot. For one thing, he lived in Brooklyn, and I'd sooner
take a trip to China. Another thing, I'm a guy that likes to eat
what I order and not what somebody deals me. And he had kids
and a wife, and the family racket is out of my line. But Hughie
looked so tickled I couldn't welsh on him. And it didn't work out
so bad. Of course, what he called home was only a dump of a cheap
flat. Still, it wasn't so bad for a change. His wife had done a lot of
stuff to doll it up. Nothin' with no class, you understand. Just
cheap stuff to make it comfortable. And his kids wasn't the gorillas
I'd expected, neither. No throwin' spitballs in my soup or them
kind of gags. They was quiet like Hughie. I kinda liked 'em. After
dinner I started tellin' 'em a story about a race horse a guy I know
owned once. I thought it was up to me to put out something, and
kids like animal stories, and this one was true, at that. This old
turtle never wins a race, but he was as foxy as ten guys, a natural
born crook, the goddamnedest thief, he'd steal anything in reach
that wasn't nailed down— Well, I didn't get far. Hughie's wife
butt in and stopped me cold. Told the kids it was bedtime and
hustled 'em off like I was giving 'em measles. It got my goat,
kinda. I coulda liked her—a little—if she'd give me a chance. Not
that she was nothin' Ziegfeld would want to glorify. When you
call her plain, you give her all the breaks.

Resentfully.

Well, to hell with it. She had me tagged for a bum, and seein' me made her sure she was right. You can bet she told Hughie never invite me again, and he never did. He tried to apologize, but I shut him up quick. He says, "Irma was brought up strict. She can't help being narrow-minded about gamblers." I said, "What's it to me? I don't want to hear your dame troubles. I got plenty of my own. Remember that doll I brung home night before last? She gives me an argument I promised her ten bucks. I told her, 'Listen, Baby, I got an impediment in my speech. Maybe it sounded like ten, but it was two, and that's all you get. Hell, I don't want to buy your soul! What would I do with it?' Now she's peddling the news along Broadway I'm a rat and a chiseler, and of course all the rats and chiselers believe her. Before she's through, I won't have a friend left."

He pauses—confidentially.

I switched the subject on Hughie, see, on purpose. He never did beef to me about his wife again.

He gives a forced chuckle.

Believe me, Pal, I can stop guys that start telling me their family troubles!

NIGHT CLERK

His mind has hopped an ambulance clanging down Sixth, and is asking without curiosity: "Will he die, Doctor, or isn't he lucky?" "I'm afraid not, but he'll have to be absolutely quiet for months and months." "With a pretty nurse taking care of him?" "Probably not pretty." "Well, anyway, I claim he's lucky. And now I must get back to the hotel. 492 won't go to bed and insists on telling me jokes. It must have been a joke because he's chuckling." He laughs with a heartiness which has for-

gotten that heart is more than a word used in "Have a heart," an old slang expression.

Ha— Ha! That's a good one, Erie. That's the best I've heard in a long time!

ERIE

For a moment is so hurt and depressed he hasn't the spirit to make a sarcastic crack. He stares at the floor, twirling his room key—to himself.

Jesus, this sure is a dead dump. About as homey as the Morgue.

He glances up at the clock.

Gettin' late. Better beat it up to my cell and grab some shut eye.

He makes a move to detach himself from the desk but fails and remains wearily glued to it. His eyes prowl the lobby and finally come to rest on the Clerk's glistening, sallow face. He summons up strength for a withering crack.

Why didn't you tell me you was deef, Buddy? I know guys is sensitive about them little afflictions, but I'll keep it confidential.

But the Clerk's mind has rushed out to follow the siren wail of a fire engine. "A fireman's life must be exciting." His mind rides the engine, and asks a fireman with disinterested eagerness: "Where's the fire? Is it a real good one this time? Has it a good start? Will it be big enough, do you think?" Erie examines his face—bitingly.

Take my tip, Pal, and don't never try to buy from a dope peddler. He'll tell you you had enough already.

The Clerk's mind continues its dialogue with the fireman: "I mean, big enough to burn down the whole damn city?" "Sorry, Brother, but there's no chance. There's too much stone and steel. There'd always be something left." "Yes, I guess you're right. There's too much stone and steel. I wasn't really hoping, anyway. It really doesn't matter to

27

me." Erie gives him up and again attempts to pry him-
self from the desk, twirling his key frantically as if it
were a fetish which might set him free.

Well, me for the hay.

But he can't dislodge himself—dully.

Christ, it's lonely. I wish Hughie was here. By God, if he was, I'd
tell him a tale that'd make his eyes pop! The bigger the story the
harder he'd fall. He was that kind of sap. He thought gambling
was romantic. I guess he saw me like a sort of dream guy, the sort
of guy he'd like to be if he could take a chance. I guess he lived a
sort of double life listening to me gabbin' about hittin' the high
spots. Come to figger it, I'll bet he even cheated on his wife that
way, using me and my dolls.

He chuckles.

No wonder he liked me, huh? And the bigger I made myself the
more he lapped it up. I went easy on him at first. I didn't lie—not
any more'n a guy naturally does when he gabs about the bets he
wins and the dolls he's made. But I soon see he was cryin' for more,
and when a sucker cries for more, you're a dope if you don't let
him have it. Every tramp I made got to be a Follies' doll. Hughie
liked 'em to be Follies' dolls. Or in the Scandals or Frolics. He
wanted me to be the Sheik of Araby, or something that any
blonde 'd go round-heeled about. Well, I give him plenty of that.
And I give him plenty of gambling tales. I explained my campin'
in this dump was because I don't want to waste jack on nothin'
but gambling. It was like dope to me, I told him. I couldn't quit.
He lapped that up. He liked to kid himself I'm mixed up in the
racket. He thought gangsters was romantic. So I fed him some
baloney about highjacking I'd done once. I told him I knew all
the Big Shots. Well, so I do, most of 'em, to say hello, and sometimes they hello back. Who wouldn't know 'em that hangs around
Broadway and the joints? I run errands for 'em sometimes, because

there's dough in it, but I'm cagey about gettin' in where it ain't healthy. Hughie wanted to think me and Legs Diamond was old pals. So I give him that too. I give him anything he cried for.

Earnestly.

Don't get the wrong idea, Pal. What I fed Hughie wasn't all lies. The tales about gambling wasn't. They was stories of big games and killings that really happened since I've been hangin' round. Only I wasn't in on 'em like I made out—except one or two from way back when I had a run of big luck and was in the bucks for a while until I was took to the cleaners.

He stops to pay tribute of a sigh to the memory of brave days that were and that never were—then meditatively.

Yeah, Hughie lapped up my stories like they was duck soup, or a beakful of heroin. I sure took him around with me in tales and showed him one hell of a time.

He chuckles—then seriously.

And, d'you know, it done me good, too, in a way. Sure. I'd get to seein' myself like he seen me. Some nights I'd come back here without a buck, feeling lower than a snake's belly, and first thing you know I'd be lousy with jack, bettin' a grand a race. Oh, I was wise I was kiddin' myself. I ain't a sap. But what the hell, Hughie loved it, and it didn't cost nobody nothin', and if every guy along Broadway who kids himself was to drop dead there wouldn't be nobody left. Ain't it the truth, Charlie?

He again stares at the Night Clerk appealingly, forgetting past rebuffs. The Clerk's face is taut with vacancy. His mind has been trying to fasten itself to some noise in the night, but a rare and threatening pause of silence has fallen on the city, and here he is, chained behind a hotel desk forever, awake when everyone else in the world is asleep, except Room 492, and he won't go to bed, he's still talking, and there is no escape.

His glassy eyes stare through Erie's face. He stammers deferentially.

Truth? I'm afraid I didn't get— What's the truth?

ERIE

Hopelessly.

Nothing, Pal. Not a thing.

His eyes fall to the floor. For a while he is too defeated even to twirl his room key. The Clerk's mind still cannot make a getaway because the city remains silent, and the night vaguely reminds him of death, and he is vaguely frightened, and now that he remembers, his feet are giving him hell, but that's no excuse not to act as if the Guest is always right: "I should have paid 492 more attention. After all, he is company. He is awake and alive. I should use him to help me live through the night. What's he been talking about? I must have caught some of it without meaning to." The Night Clerk's forehead puckers perspiringly as he tries to remember. Erie begins talking again but this time it is obviously aloud to himself, without hope of a listener.

I could tell by Hughie's face before he went to the hospital, he was through. I've seen the same look on guys' faces when they knew they was on the spot, just before guys caught up with them. I went to see him twice in the hospital. The first time, his wife was there and give me a dirty look, but he cooked up a smile and said, "Hello, Erie, how're the bangtails treating you?" I see he wants a big story to cheer him, but his wife butts in and says he's weak and he mustn't get excited. I felt like crackin', "Well, the Docs in this dump got the right dope. Just leave you with him and he'll never get excited." The second time I went, they wouldn't let me see him. That was near the end. I went to his funeral, too. There wasn't nobody but a coupla his wife's relations. I had to feel sorry for her. She looked like she ought to be parked in a coffin, too. The kids was bawlin'. There wasn't no flowers but a coupla lousy wreaths. It woulda been a punk showing for poor old Hughie, if it hadn't been for my flower piece.

He swells with pride.

That was some display, Pal. It'd knock your eye out! Set me back a hundred bucks, and no kiddin'! A big horseshoe of red roses! I knew Hughie'd want a horseshoe because that made it look like he'd been a horse player. And around the top printed in forget-me-nots was "Good-by, Old Pal." Hughie liked to kid himself he was my pal.

He adds sadly.

And so he was, at that—even if he was a sucker.

> *He pauses, his false poker face as nakedly forlorn as an organ grinder's monkey's. Outside, the spell of abnormal quiet presses suffocatingly upon the street, enters the deserted, dirty lobby. The Night Clerk's mind cowers away from it. He cringes behind the desk, his feet aching like hell. There is only one possible escape. If his mind could only fasten onto something 492 has said.* "What's he been talking about? A clerk should always be attentive. You even are duty bound to laugh at a guest's smutty jokes, no matter how often you've heard them. That's the policy of the hotel. 492 has been gassing for hours. What's he been telling me? I must be slipping. Always before this I've been able to hear without bothering to listen, but now when I need company— Ah! I've got it! Gambling! He said a lot about gambling. That's something I've always wanted to know more about, too. Maybe he's a professional gambler. Like Arnold Rothstein."

NIGHT CLERK

Blurts out with an uncanny, almost lifelike eagerness.

I beg your pardon, Mr.—Erie—but did I understand you to say you are a gambler by profession? Do you, by any chance, know the Big Shot, Arnold Rothstein?

> *But this time it is Erie who doesn't hear him. And the Clerk's mind is now suddenly impervious to the threat of Night and Silence as it pursues an ideal of fame and glory within itself called Arnold Rothstein.*

ERIE

With mournful longing.

Christ, I wish Hughie was alive and kickin'. I'd tell him I win ten grand from the bookies, and ten grand at stud, and ten grand in a crap game! I'd tell him I bought one of those Mercedes sport roadsters with nickel pipes sticking out of the hood! I'd tell him I lay three babes from the Follies—two blondes and one brunette!

> *The Night Clerk dreams, a rapt hero worship transfiguring his pimply face: "Arnold Rothstein! He must be some guy! I read a story about him. He'll gamble for any limit on anything, and always wins. The story said he wouldn't bother playing in a poker game unless the smallest bet you could make—one white chip!—was a hundred dollars. Christ, that's going some! I'd like to have the dough to get in a game with him once! The last pot everyone would drop out but him and me. I'd say, 'Okay, Arnold, the sky's the limit,' and I'd raise him five grand, and he'd call, and I'd have a royal flush to his four aces. Then I'd say, 'Okay, Arnold, I'm a good sport, I'll give you a break. I'll cut you double or nothing. Just one cut. I want quick action for my dough.' And I'd cut the ace of spades and win again." Beatific vision swoons on the empty pools of the Night Clerk's eyes. He*

resembles a holy saint, recently elected to Paradise. Erie breaks the silence—bitterly resigned.

But Hughie's better off, at that, being dead. He's got all the luck. He needn't do no worryin' now. He's out of the racket. I mean, the whole goddamned racket. I mean life.

> NIGHT CLERK
> *Kicked out of his dream—with detached, pleasant acquiescence.*

Yes, it is a goddamned racket when you stop to think, isn't it, 492? But we might as well make the best of it, because— Well, you can't burn it all down, can you? There's too much steel and stone. There'd always be something left to start it going again.

> ERIE
> *Scowls bewilderedly.*

Say, what is this? What the hell you talkin' about?

> NIGHT CLERK
> *At a loss—in much confusion.*

Why, to be frank, I really don't— Just something that came into my head.

> ERIE
> *Bitingly, but showing he is comforted at having made some sort of contact.*

Get it out of your head quick, Charlie, or some guys in uniform will walk in here with a butterfly net and catch you.

He changes the subject—earnestly.

Listen, Pal, maybe you guess I was kiddin' about that flower piece for Hughie costing a hundred bucks? Well, I ain't! I didn't give a damn what it cost. It was up to me to give Hughie a big-time send-off, because I knew nobody else would.

Oh, I'm not doubting your word, Erie. You won the money gambling, I suppose— I mean, I beg your pardon if I'm mistaken, but you are a gambler, aren't you?

ERIE

Preoccupied.

Yeah, sure, when I got scratch to put up. What of it? But I don't win that hundred bucks. I don't win a bet since Hughie was took to the hospital. I had to get down on my knees and beg every guy I know for a sawbuck here and a sawbuck there until I raised it.

NIGHT CLERK

His mind concentrated on the Big Ideal—insistently.

Do you by any chance know—Arnold Rothstein?

ERIE

His train of thought interrupted—irritably.

Arnold? What's he got to do with it? He wouldn't loan a guy like me a nickel to save my grandmother from streetwalking.

NIGHT CLERK

With humble awe.

Then you do know him!

ERIE

Sure I know the bastard. Who don't on Broadway? And he knows me—when he wants to. He uses me to run errands when there ain't no one else handy. But he ain't my trouble, Pal. My trouble is, some of these guys I put the bite on is dead wrong G's, and they expect to be paid back next Tuesday, or else I'm outa luck and have to take it on the lam, or I'll get beat up and maybe sent to a hospital.

> *He suddenly rouses himself and there is something pathetically but genuinely gallant about him.*

34

But what the hell. I was wise I was takin' a chance. I've always took a chance, and if I lose I pay, and no welshing! It sure was worth it to give Hughie the big send-off.

> *He pauses. The Night Clerk hasn't paid any attention except to his own dream. A question is trembling on his parted lips, but before he can get it out Erie goes on gloomily.*

But even that ain't my big worry, Charlie. My big worry is the run of bad luck I've had since Hughie got took to the hospital. Not a win. That ain't natural. I've always been a lucky guy— lucky enough to get by and pay up, I mean. I wouldn't never worry about owing guys, like I owe them guys. I'd always know I'd make a win that'd fix it. But now I got a lousy hunch when I lost Hughie I lost my luck—I mean, I've lost the old confidence. He used to give me confidence.

> *He turns away from the desk.*

No use gabbin' here all night. You can't do me no good.

> *He starts toward the elevator.*

NIGHT CLERK
> *Pleadingly.*

Just a minute, Erie, if you don't mind.

> *With awe.*

So you're an old friend of Arnold Rothstein! Would you mind telling me if it's really true when Arnold Rothstein plays poker, one white chip is—a hundred dollars?

ERIE
> *Dully exasperated.*

Say, for Christ's sake, what's it to you— ?

> *He stops abruptly, staring probingly at the Clerk. There is a pause. Suddenly his face lights up with a saving revelation. He grins warmly and saunters confidently back to the desk.*

35

Say, Charlie, why didn't you put me wise before, you was interested in gambling? Hell, I got you all wrong, Pal. I been tellin' myself, this guy ain't like old Hughie. He ain't got no sportin' blood. He's just a dope.

> *Generously.*

Now I see you're a right guy. Shake.

> *He shoves out his hand which the Clerk clasps with a limp pleasure. Erie goes on with gathering warmth and self-assurance.*

That's the stuff. You and me'll get along. I'll give you all the breaks, like I give Hughie.

> NIGHT CLERK
>
> *Gratefully.*

Thank you, Erie.

> *Then insistently.*

Is it true when Arnold Rothstein plays poker, one white chip—

> ERIE
>
> *With magnificent carelessness.*

Sets you back a hundred bucks? Sure. Why not? Arnold's in the bucks, ain't he? And when you're in the bucks, a C note is chicken feed. I ought to know, Pal. I was in the bucks when Arnold was a piker. Why, one time down in New Orleans I lit a cigar with a C note, just for a gag, y'understand. I was with a bunch of high class dolls and I wanted to see their eyes pop out—and believe me, they sure popped! After that, I coulda made 'em one at a time or all together! Hell, I once win twenty grand on a single race. That's action! A good crap game is action, too. Hell, I've been in games where there was a hundred grand in real folding money lying around the floor. That's travelin'!

> *He darts a quick glance at the Clerk's face and begins to hedge warily. But he needn't. The Clerk sees him now*

as the Gambler in 492, the Friend of Arnold Rothstein—
and nothing is incredible. Erie goes on.

Of course, I wouldn't kid you. I'm not in the bucks now—not right this moment. You know how it is, Charlie. Down today and up tomorrow. I got some dough ridin' on the nose of a turtle in the 4th at Saratoga. I hear a story he'll be so full of hop, if the joc can keep him from jumpin' over the grandstand, he'll win by a mile. So if I roll in here with a blonde that'll knock your eyes out, don't be surprised.

He winks and chuckles.

NIGHT CLERK
Ingratiatingly pally, smiling.

Oh, you can't surprise me that way. I've been a night clerk in New York all my life, almost.

He tries out a wink himself.

I'll forget the house rules, Erie.

ERIE
Dryly.

Yeah. The manager wouldn't like you to remember something he ain't heard of yet.

Then slyly feeling his way.

How about shootin' a little crap, Charlie? I mean just in fun, like I used to with Hughie. I know you can't afford takin' no chances. I'll stake you, see? I got a coupla bucks. We gotta use real jack or it don't look real. It's all my jack, get it? You can't lose. I just want to show you how I'll take you to the cleaners. It'll give me confidence.

He has taken two one-dollar bills and some change from his pocket. He pushes most of it across to the Clerk.

Here y'are.

He produces a pair of dice—carelessly.

Want to give these dice the once-over before we start?

NIGHT CLERK
Earnestly.

What do you think I am? I know I can trust you.

ERIE
Smiles.

You remind me a lot of Hughie, Pal. He always trusted me. Well, don't blame me if I'm lucky.

He clicks the dice in his hand—thoughtfully.

Y'know, it's time I quit carryin' the torch for Hughie. Hell, what's the use? It don't do him no good. He's gone. Like we all gotta go. Him yesterday, me or you tomorrow, and who cares, and what's the difference? It's all in the racket, huh?

His soul is purged of grief, his confidence restored.

I shoot two bits.

NIGHT CLERK
Manfully, with an excited dead-pan expression he hopes resembles Arnold Rothstein's.

I fade you.

ERIE
Throws the dice.

Four's my point.

Gathers them up swiftly and throws them again.

Four it is.

He takes the money.

Easy when you got my luck—and know how. Huh, Charlie?

He chuckles, giving the Night Clerk the slyly amused, contemptuous, affectionate wink with which a Wise Guy regales a Sucker.

CURTAIN